BEYOND HORIZONS

VERSES OF ADVENTURE

"The poems nostalgically illustrate a man's journey of life and the yearning to explore the unknown within and without!"
PADMA BHUSHAN DR. (MRS.) SHAYAMA CHONA

GOPAL KUMAR

ISBN

Hardcase 979-8-89322-777-2
Paperback 979-8-89277-554-0

Dedicated to

My mother, Dr. (Mrs.) Pushpa Tiwari,
because of whom I exist

And to

Saurabh Agarwal and Priyanka Singh Agarwal,
for always being there

Contents

Prologue: Beyond Horizons – Verses of Adventure

In the heart of Bihar, where the Ganges meanders through tales of resilience, and in the modest city of Muzaffarpur, a captivating story unfolded against the backdrop of economic constraints and underdevelopment. Born into a landscape where aspirations often contend with the harsh realities of a region marked by the lowest GDP per capita in India, the author found champions in an unwavering mother and a wise grandfather. Their belief, a beacon amidst challenges, set the stage for a narrative that would transcend boundaries and expectations.

The odyssey commenced on June 5, 2007, soaring from the bustling cityscape of New Delhi to the iconic skyline of New York. It was more than a mere journey; it was a pilgrimage of education and opportunity, a transformative expedition that held profound significance beyond the geographical traverse. The destination was Cambridge, Massachusetts, where the historic walls of Harvard University bore witness to a commencement ceremony graced by the wisdom of Bill Gates.

As the author stepped onto the global stage, it marked the beginning of a journey that would unfold over the next thirteen years—a journey encapsulated in the anthology that is "Beyond Horizons – Verses of Adventure." This collection, now more than a mere collection of poems, is a reflection of a life lived on the edges of expectation, embracing the unpredictability of exploration.

From the hallowed halls of Harvard to the vibrant streets of Singapore, academia became the gateway to a global sojourn. The Lion City, in 2008, became a second home, the backdrop to a myriad of experiences that expanded not just the horizons on maps but also those within the heart. Each step, each encounter, and each cultural immersion became threads woven into the fabric of an unfolding adventure.

The verses in this collection, crafted with the finesse of a seasoned traveler, are not just poetic expressions; they are the brushstrokes on the canvas of a life well-lived. Yet, this journey was not without its challenges—challenges that transcended the ordinary. Since September 2002, the author has faced the daily trials of Type 1 Diabetes, a relentless companion that demanded four injections each day. The perpetual shadow of this condition, however, did not cast darkness but rather illuminated the path with a unique radiance.

Each day became a testament to resilience, a defiance of limitations that, to many, might have seemed insurmountable. And so, amidst the towering spires of academia, the bustling markets of distant lands, and the serene landscapes that whispered tales of their own, the author stood not as a victim of circumstance but as a triumphant navigator of an unconventional path.

The rhythm of the verses in "Beyond Horizons" echoes the essence of a transformative journey—one that transcends mere geographical coordinates. The journey is a kaleidoscope of experiences, a celebration of resilience, an homage to the transformative power of education, and an anthem to the indomitable spirit of adventure. The tales within these verses unfold as chapters of a narrative where the compass of possibility is not bound by one's background or circumstances.

Fasten your seatbelt, dear reader, for within the pages of "Beyond Horizons – Verses of Adventure," lies an invitation to traverse landscapes both literal and metaphorical. The adventure unfolded until the unexpected arrival of the coronavirus, a global disruption that brought with it a pause, a reflection, and an opportunity to distil the essence of the journey so far.

This collection is not merely about the places visited; it is about the people encountered, the lessons learned, and the personal evolution that transpired. It is an odyssey of self-discovery, of finding home in the unfamiliar, and of realizing that the journey itself is a destination.

In this expansive canvas of words, feel the heartbeat of the journey, sense the fragrance of the places explored, and hear the whispers of the stories untold. "Beyond Horizons – Verses of Adventure" is not just a collection of poems; it is an immersive experience, an exploration of the extraordinary within the ordinary, and an invitation to join the author in a dance with the unknown. So, with anticipation and curiosity, step into the pages that await, and let the adventure begin anew. And as this narrative unfolds, remember that the greatest assets accumulated at the end of this journey are not material possessions but experiences captured in three passports, with each page filled with stamps that tell tales of a life lived beyond horizons.

"Wanderlust's Awakening" – A Longing to Explore the World

In dreams, I see a world unfurled,
Where distant lands, their flags unfurl,
And wanderlust, like flames, it burns,
A fervent thirst, a heart that yearns.

To traverse mountains, valleys wide,
To sail the seas, be by the tide,
To walk through forests, ancient, grand,
And touch the earth in every land.

The whispered tales of far-off places,
Draw me with their wondrous graces,
From bustling cities to quiet glades,
In every corner, in sun and shades.

The unknown roads, they call to me,
A siren's song, wild and free,
With each new dawn, my spirit shakes,
To see the world, for wanderlust's sake.

To taste the cultures, hear their stories,
In foreign tongues, find hidden glories,
To understand, to bridge divides,
In travel's dance, my soul abides.

Oh, wanderlust, my constant guide,
In you, my dreams take form and stride,
To explore the world, both near and far,
In your embrace, I find my star.

"A Road Less Traveled" – Embracing the Unconventional Path

Beneath the canopy of life, I tread,
Upon a path less worn, where others seldom thread,
No well-trodden way, no footprints to trace,
I embrace the unknown with a hopeful grace.

Through tangled woods and uncharted lands,
I find strength in choices where the heart understands,
The beauty of divergence, the unconventional way,
Where new perspectives bloom in the light of day.

The road less travelled, an untamed domain,
Where innovation thrives and free spirits reign,
It beckons with whispers, with promises unknown,
As I walk this path, I've truly grown.

With courage in my heart and dreams in my stride,
I'll carve my own way, with nothing to hide,
For in these uncharted steps, I find my bliss,
Embracing the unconventional, in every moment's kiss.

"The Odyssey of Dreams" – Exploring the Power of Imagination

In dreams, I sail on ships of starlight's gleam,
Through boundless skies, in an endless dream,
The power of imagination, a force so grand,
Unfolds the world at my command.

I journey through realms both near and far,
Beyond the limits of sun and star,
With every thought, a new world takes flight,
Guided by the beacon of creative light.

In dreams, I build castles from whispers of air,
With turrets of wonder and bridges to where,
The impossible meets the conceivable shore,
In the realm where fantasies endlessly pour.

I delve into mysteries, weave tales untold,
With characters vivid, both young and old,
In the odyssey of dreams, I find my muse,
A treasure trove of thoughts to amuse.

Through realms of thought, my spirit soars,
As imagination's magic opens new doors,
In the theatre of dreams, I take the stage,
A playwright, actor, and audience in this age.

The tapestry of fantasies we artfully weave,
Through visions and dreams, we truly believe,
That the power of imagination knows no bounds,
A universe of wonders in each thought's surrounds.

So, let us dream on, let our visions ignite,
For in the odyssey of dreams, we take flight,
Exploring the cosmos of creative streams,
Forever enchanted by imagination's gleams.

"Journey to the Horizon" – The Allure of the Unknown

In shadows cast by setting sun's descent,
I start a journey to the horizon's extent,
Drawn by the mystic pull of the unknown,
To lands uncharted, where seeds are sown.

The allure of distant shores, a siren's call,
In the twilight's embrace, I give my all,
With every step, my heart's aglow,
To chase the sun's last golden glow.

Over hills and valleys, I'll venture far,
Beneath the canvas of the evening star,
Through darkness and through light, I roam,
For the horizon's promise feels like home.

Though the path ahead may twist and bend,
I'll follow it to where my dreams ascend,
In the journey to the horizon, I find my grace,
Embracing the allure of the unknown's embrace.

"Wandering Through Time" – Reflecting on the Past During a Journey

As I wander through time on this path unknown,
Reflections of the past like seeds are sown,
Each step I take, a page turned in history's rhyme,
In the embrace of memories, I wander through time.

The echoes of laughter, the tears that have dried,
In the footsteps of yesteryears, I confide,
With every stride forward, I glance back to see,
The moments that shaped me, the person I'd be.

Through fields of nostalgia, I gently wade,
In the river of remembrance, where stories are laid,
Faces and places, once vivid and real,
Now woven in whispers that time cannot steal.

In the stillness of moments, I pause and reflect,
On the lessons of life, the joys and the wrecked,
For in wandering through time, I find my own grace,
A journey through history, a heartwarming embrace.

So, I'll walk this path with my memories in tow,
With gratitude and reverence, to the past I'll bestow,
For in wandering through time, I discover the prime,
Of life's endless tapestry, in this wondrous climb.

"Voyage of Discovery" – The Joy of Uncovering New Experiences

Upon the vessel of my dreams, I set sail,
In a voyage of discovery, I shall not fail,
With an eager heart and a fearless soul,
I embark on a journey, my destiny to unroll.

The world's a treasure chest, full of surprises untold,
Each adventure, a gem, a story to be bold,
With open eyes, I embrace the unknown,
In the voyage of discovery, my spirit has grown.

Through uncharted waters, I navigate with glee,
The thrill of exploration, a melody to me,
New horizons beckon, and I gladly obey,
For in every discovery, life finds its own way.

The taste of new flavors, the scent of the sea,
The touch of foreign lands, where my heart wants to be,
With every step ashore, I leave footprints behind,
In the sands of memory, an impression defined.

From the peaks of mountains to the depths of the sea,
The voyage of discovery sets my spirit free,
In the heart of the moment, I find my true bliss,
As I uncover new worlds, with a passionate kiss.

The cultures I encounter, the souls I befriend,
In the voyage of discovery, I mend and amend,
For every experience, every encounter, every chance,
Is a piece of life's puzzle, a graceful, wild dance.

In the voyage of discovery, I learn and I grow,
As the river of time continues to flow,
With each dawn that breaks, a new day to seize,
In this grand expedition, where joy never cease.

So, onward I sail, in the wake of the sun,
In the voyage of discovery, where my journey's begun,
With wonder in my heart and a twinkle in my eye,
I cherish each moment, as time passes by.

"Nomadic Soul" – The Restless Spirit of the Traveller

A nomadic soul, forever on the roam,
In the heart of wanderlust, it finds its home,
Restless as the wind, it seeks the unknown,
In the footprints of the world, its seeds are sown.

Unfettered by borders, unchained by the land,
It craves the freedom of the endless sand,
A seeker of horizons, both near and far,
It follows its dreams, like a distant star.

In foreign tongues, it finds its melody,
As it dances to rhythms of life's tapestry,
A nomadic soul, guided by the stars above,
In its boundless quest, it finds its true love.

Through city streets and wilderness uncharted,
Its spirit soars, forever unparted,
For it's in the journey, in the endless quest,
That the nomadic soul finds its deepest rest.

Though the road is long and the night is dark,
The nomadic soul leaves its indelible mark,
In the stories it tells and the lives it has known,
A nomadic soul, forever on its own.

With each sunrise, it's reborn anew,
In the open road's embrace, dreams come true,
A wanderer, a dreamer, free and whole,
Forever guided by its nomadic soul.

"A Roadside Epiphany" – Finding Inspiration in Unexpected Places

Beside a winding road, where wildflowers sway,
A moment of epiphany found its way,
In the simplest of places, amidst nature's grace,
A roadside revelation took its place.

I wandered, lost in thought, my mind a haze,
When nature's beauty met my wandering gaze,
The sun dipped low, a canvas of gold and red,
In that fleeting hour, inspiration spread.

The rustling leaves whispered secrets untold,
In the language of the wind, my heart was consoled,
Each wildflower a brushstroke, each tree a frame,
A roadside masterpiece in nature's name.

I realized then, in that tranquil space,
Inspiration finds us in every place,
In the unexpected moments, the ordinary scene,
A roadside epiphany, a chance to dream.

The world's a gallery, open and wide,
Where inspiration resides, in each stride,
So let us wander, with open hearts and eyes,
For roadside epiphanies are life's sweetest surprise.

In the midst of the mundane, the daily grind,
A roadside revelation, a gift to the mind,
For in these unexpected spaces, we often find,
That inspiration blossoms, in the soul's design.

"The Call of the Open Road" – Embracing the Freedom of Travel

In the silence of the morning's hush,
I heed the call, a gentle, thrilling rush,
The open road before me, boundless, wide,
In its whispered promise, I long to ride.

With a heart unburdened, I take the lead,
Embracing freedom, a profound need,
The wind in my hair, the world in my view,
The open road, an endless avenue.

No maps to bind me, no schedules to meet,
I'll chase the horizon, with eager feet,
The highway's song, a melody so sweet,
In the call of the open road, my soul finds its beat.

Through rolling hills and valleys low,
Wherever the journey leads, I'll go,
With every mile, a story unfolds,
In the tapestry of life, its threads and its folds.

The sun on my face, the breeze at my side,
In the journey's embrace, I'll let nothing hide,
For the open road is where my spirit's free,
Embracing its call, my heart's jubilee.

So, let me wander, let me explore,
On the open road, I'll find what's in store,
In the embrace of travel, I am whole,
As I answer the call of the open road's soul.

"Footprints in the Sand" – Leaving One's Mark on the World

Upon the shores of time, we walk the land,
Leaving footprints in the sand, grains of life's grand,
In every step we take, a story's told,
As footprints in the sand, they never grow old.

Some may be light, like whispers in the breeze,
Others deep and lasting, like ancient trees,
Each one unique, a testament to our stay,
Footprints in the sand, marking life's highway.

They speak of where we've been, the paths we've trod,
The joys and sorrows, the moments with God,
A trace of our journey, both near and far,
Footprints in the sand, a memoir, a memoir.

In the tides of time, they may fade away,
But the echoes of our presence will forever sway,
For though we may move on, to new, unknown lands,
Our footprints in the sand, remain as love's strands.

As we journey through life, let's tread with care,
Leaving footprints of kindness, showing we care,
For in the end, it's not what we amass or demand,
But the love we've left behind, like footprints in the sand.

So, let us walk with purpose, let our hearts expand,
Leaving a legacy of love, like footprints in the sand,
In the sands of time, where all life's stories blend,
May our footprints in the sand, be a message to send.

"Roaming Through Memories" – Nostalgia and Reflection on Past Journeys

Roaming through memories, a timeless embrace,
In the sepia of recollection, I find my special place,
With each cherished moment, a journey unfurls,
Nostalgia's sweet melody, like the strings of pearls.

I stroll down old streets, paved with yesteryears,
Where laughter and tears echo in my ears,
The scent of bygone days, so vivid and clear,
In the gardens of remembrance, I find solace here.

Through the annals of time, I wander and roam,
In the corridors of memory, I find my true home,
The tales of past journeys, etched in my heart,
Roaming through memories, where each piece is a part.

In the warmth of nostalgia, I pause and reflect,
On the treasures of life, on the love I collect,
With each step I take, I am grateful anew,
Roaming through memories, where dreams come into view.

In the quiet of reverie, where the past softly gleams,
I cherish these moments, these precious old themes,
For in roaming through memories, I am whole and complete,
Nostalgia's gentle embrace, a love song so sweet.

"Quest for the Unknown" – Seeking Adventure and New Horizons

In the heart of the brave, where dreams take flight,
A quest for the unknown, a beacon of light,
With maps uncharted and compass in hand,
We journey forth to a faraway land.

Through untamed forests and mountains so high,
In search of adventure, we'll reach for the sky,
With every step forward, a story unfolds,
A quest for the unknown, where mysteries hold.

The call of the wild, the whispers of fate,
In the thrill of the chase, we embrace the great,
Seeking new horizons, where boundaries expand,
In the quest for the unknown, we take a bold stand.

Through tempests and trials, we'll forge our own way,
In the face of the challenges, come what may,
For the heart of an explorer knows no retreat,
In the quest for the unknown, our journey's complete.

With stars as our guide and the wind as our song,
We'll travel the path where we truly belong,
In the boundless expanse, where dreams are sown,
We'll forever embark on the quest for the unknown.

"Echoes of the Journey" – Memories of Past Travels

In the silent chambers of my mind, they reside,
Echoes of the journey, memories, in them, I confide,
Each one a treasure, a moment in time,
In the vast archives of my heart, they climb.

I hear the rustling leaves in a forest so grand,
As I walked hand in hand, in a distant land,
The whispering wind from a mountaintop high,
Where I reached for the sky, with an endless sigh.

The laughter of strangers in a bustling square,
The taste of exotic spices in the vibrant air,
Footsteps on cobbled streets, echoes of the past,
In memories, these moments forever will last.

I see the ancient ruins, weathered and worn,
In the light of the dawn, where history is born,
The colours of a market, vibrant and alive,
As I dive into the hive, where cultures thrive.

I touch the cool waters of a tranquil shore,
As waves kiss the shore, and I long for more,
The warmth of a campfire on a starry night,
Underneath the moonlight, a breathtaking sight.

I taste the flavours of a foreign cuisine,
In every dish, a story, a journey unseen,
The sweetness of a shared meal with newfound friends,
In these echoes of the journey, my heart mends.

I feel the embrace of a foreign land's embrace,
In every warm smile, in every kind face,
The touch of a place where I once called home,
In these echoes of the journey, I'm never alone.

Each memory is a thread, woven in my soul,
As the years unroll, they make me whole,
In the symphony of life, they form a melodic tune,
These echoes of the journey, beneath the same moon.

In the tapestry of time, they are my cherished art,
Etched in every part of my wandering heart,
In the mosaic of moments, they forever play,
These echoes of the journey, guiding my way.

So I hold them close, these treasures of the past,
For in them, I'm steadfast, in every memory cast,
In the echoes of the journey, I'll always find,
The map of my soul, my wandering mind.

"The Wayfarer's Lament" – The Bittersweet Feeling of Leaving a Place Behind

With every step, a piece of me I leave,
The wayfarer's lament, like autumn's gentle heave,
In leaving, there's a tinge of bittersweet pain,
A heartache for the moments that won't come again.

The memories I gather, like petals in the breeze,
Are woven into my soul, with each passing tease,
As I bid farewell to the places I've known,
The wayfarer's lament, a sigh, a soft moan.

But in the parting, a promise takes root,
That in the journey ahead, I'll find the truth,
For with every goodbye, a new path unfurls,
The wayfarer's lament, a canvas of twirls.

So, I'll carry these memories, in my heart they'll reside,
As I travel forward, with dreams as my guide,
In the wayfarer's lament, I'll cherish the past,
But embrace the future, with open arms cast.

"Wanderer's Reverie" – Daydreaming About Future Travels

In moments of quiet, my mind takes flight,
To places unseen, where dreams ignite,
A wanderer's reverie, a magical trance,
Daydreaming of future, in a wild dance.

I close my eyes, and I'm swept away,
To the lands where I'll wander someday,
The cities I'll explore, the cultures I'll meet,
In this wanderer's reverie, my heart skips a beat.

I see ancient ruins bathed in golden sun,
Feel the thrill of adventure, the need to run,
The mountains I'll climb, the oceans I'll brave,
In this daydream of travels, my spirit's a wave.

Through bustling bazaars and tranquil retreats,
My wanderlust beckons, my heart competes,
With every destination, a story to find,
In this wanderer's reverie, my soul's intertwined.

I taste exotic flavors, smell fragrant blooms,
In these vivid daydreams, there's no room for gloom,
The world's a treasure, waiting to be unfurled,
In this wanderer's reverie, I'm a traveler of the world.

With open arms, I'll embrace the unknown,
Let the winds of adventure carry me on,
For in these daydreams, I find my sweet release,
A wanderer's reverie, where my soul finds its peace.

"The Odyssey of the Heart" – Love and Connection Across Distances

In the vast expanse of the world, we're apart,
Yet love knows no bounds, it's an odyssey of the heart,
Through miles and oceans that stretch far and wide,
Our love remains steadfast, a bond that won't hide.

Though separated by land, by sea, by the miles,
Our hearts are connected by a thousand shared smiles,
In the odyssey of the heart, distance can't sever,
The love that we hold, that lasts now and forever.

Through the tapestry of time, we'll find our way,
In the depths of our love, come what may,
For love transcends borders, it defies every chart,
In the odyssey of the heart, we're never truly apart.

In the silence of night, in the light of the day,
Our love's like a compass, it shows us the way,
Across the divide, in the realms we must part,
We journey together, in the odyssey of the heart.

So let's cherish this love, let it be our guide,
In the odyssey of the heart, we'll always reside,
For distance can't conquer, nor keep us apart,
In the odyssey of the heart, we are one, heart to heart

"Journey to Self-Discovery" – Finding Oneself Through Travel

Beneath the canvas of the endless sky,
I embarked on a journey, not knowing why,
To find myself in the vast unknown,
In the wilderness of life, I've grown.

Through deserts of doubt and mountains of fear,
I've faced my demons, held them near,
In the journey to self-discovery, I've found,
A deeper purpose, a solid ground.

I wandered through cultures, diverse and bright,
Learned from every soul I met in the light,
In their stories, I found fragments of my own,
In the journey to self-discovery, I've grown.

Through bustling cities and tranquil streams,
I've chased my dreams, followed my themes,
In the symphony of life, I've found my tune,
In the journey to self-discovery, I've been immune.

To doubts that whispered, to fears that jeered,
I've shed my layers, my spirit steered,
In the tapestry of existence, I've been sewn,
In the journey to self-discovery, I've known.

Through the seasons of joy and winters of strife,
I've carved my path, painted my life,
In the mosaic of moments, I've shone,
In the journey to self-discovery, I've found home.

So let us wander, let us explore,
In the depths of our souls, we'll find much more,
In the journey to self-discovery, we'll rise and soar,
As we embrace the unknown, forevermore.

"Whispers of the Wind" – The Stories Carried by the Breeze

In the quiet of the evening, as the day takes its leave,
I listen to the whispers of the wind, in them, I believe,
For in their gentle sighs, stories are entwined,
In the whispers of the wind, secrets of all kind.

They tell of ancient trees, with branches reaching high,
Whispering tales of centuries, against the endless sky,
Of lovers who met in twilight's tender grace,
In the whispers of the wind, love finds its place.

They carry the laughter of children at play,
As they run through meadows, in the warmth of the day,
The wind's sweet serenade, a playful, joyful tune,
In the whispers of the wind, youth finds its monsoon.

They bring echoes of far-off lands, foreign and unknown,
Where cultures intertwine, their stories softly sewn,
From distant shores and cities, their essence takes a ride,
In the whispers of the wind, diversity stands with pride.

They share the sorrows of souls, burdened and frail,
In moments of despair, when hope sets sail,
The wind carries their burdens, a compassionate embrace,
In the whispers of the wind, solace finds its space.

They hold the wisdom of the ages, lessons from the past,
In their ancient melodies, traditions that will last,
A testament to history, where knowledge is enshrined,
In the whispers of the wind, wisdom's vine is twined.

They sing of dreams, of futures yet untold,
As they whisper through the night, in the stories they unfold,
In the hearts of dreamers, their melodies take flight,
In the whispers of the wind, dreams find their might.

So, in the hush of twilight, as the world settles in,
I listen to the whispers of the wind, where stories begin,
For in their gentle murmurs, the world's tales reside,
In the whispers of the wind, life's symphony does glide.

"Voyage of the Imagination" – Where Creativity and Travel Intersect

In the voyage of the imagination, I set sail,
Beyond the boundaries of reality's veil,
With the compass of creativity, I chart my course,
To distant realms, where art finds its source.

Through the corridors of the mind, I explore,
In the landscapes of dreams, I seek to implore,
The colors and textures that life can provide,
In the voyage of the imagination, where worlds coincide.

I journey through words, like a poet's quill,
In the verses and stanzas, where emotions distill,
I paint with the palette of thoughts, vivid and bright,
In the voyage of the imagination, my inner world takes flight.

Through the lens of the artist, I capture the view,
In strokes of the brush, where visions come true,
I sculpt with ideas, like a sculptor's hand,
In the voyage of the imagination, where visions expand.

I dance with the characters, in stories untold,
In the pages of books, where adventures unfold,
I compose with the music of feelings and sound,
In the voyage of the imagination, creativity is found.

Through the tapestry of thoughts, I weave and design,
In the patterns of dreams, where concepts align,
I build worlds anew, where innovation prevails,
In the voyage of the imagination, my creativity sails.

With every creation, a journey's begun,
In the voyage of the imagination, there's always more to be done,
For the intersection of travel and creativity is where I reside,
In the voyage of the imagination, my spirit's guide.

"Nomad's Song" – A Tribute to the Wandering Spirit

In the heart of a wanderer, a fire does burn,
A nomad's soul, forever on the turn,
From dusty roads to oceans wide and free,
The world's a canvas, where dreams are set free.

With a backpack and dreams, they take the lead,
In search of adventures, new places to heed,
No boundaries can bind them, no walls confine,
A nomad's heart, with horizons as its shrine.

Through sunsets and dawns, they march on and on,
Their footsteps a dance, to a nomad's song,
In the call of the open road, they find their grace,
A nomad's journey, an endless embrace.

They sleep under stars, 'neath the moon's soft glow,
In the wilderness, where wild rivers flow,
Through deserts of sand, and mountains so high,
A nomad's spirit, forever will fly.

With strangers they share tales, laughter, and strife,
In the tapestry of humanity, they find life,
With each new face, a connection so deep,
A nomad's heart, in these bonds, it does keep.

They learn from the cultures, they meet on their way,
In the melting pot of life, they find their own say,
With every encounter, a lesson to hold,
A nomad's wisdom, in these stories, it's told.

Through bustling bazaars and tranquil retreats,
They taste life's flavours, savouring each sweet,
In the cuisines of the world, a feast of delight,
A nomad's journey, a culinary flight.

They chase the horizon, where dreams take form,
In the promise of the unknown, they weather the storm,
With courage in their hearts, they navigate the vast,
A nomad's quest, from the first to the last.

Through hardships they grow, through moments of grace,
In the trials of travel, they find their place,
With each challenge faced, they become strong,
A nomad's resilience, a lifelong song.

With a camera in hand, they capture the view,
In the lens of the world, they find what's true,
In the beauty they frame, in every photo's lore,
A nomad's vision, in these pictures, it'll soar.

In the solitude of nature, they find their retreat,
In the forest's embrace, or by the ocean's beat,
With every sunset, every sunrise's glow,
A nomad's solace, in these moments, they'll know.

Through seasons they wander, through landscapes they roam,
In the nomad's heart, the world is their home,
With every journey, a story unfolds long,
A nomad's legacy, in the wanderer's song.

So here's to the nomads, to their spirit so free,
In the heart of a wanderer, let it forever be,
With each step they take, with every path they trod,
In the nomad's soul, the world finds its nod.

"The Road Less Taken" – Embracing Unique Paths in Life

Upon the road less taken, I set my stride,
Where twists and turns in shadows hide,
A path untraveled, a journey unknown,
In the realm of uniqueness, I've grown.

The world's familiar routes, they beckon near,
But I choose the uncharted, without fear,
For in the untrodden, I find my own way,
Embracing uniqueness, come what may.

The road less taken, a canvas so wide,
Where dreams and passions forever reside,
I'll leave my mark on this winding track,
In the embrace of difference, I'll never look back.

The choices I make, the risks I bear,
In the road less taken, I find what's rare,
For in the distinct, the extraordinary unfolds,
Embracing uniqueness, my spirit enrols.

So, here I go, down this path of my choosing,
With courage and hope, there's no losing,
Upon the road less taken, my heart's awakened,
In the symphony of uniqueness, my soul's unshaken.

"A Stranger's Smile" – The Warmth of Human Connection in Foreign Lands

In a foreign land, where I roam and roam,
A stranger's smile becomes my heart's sweet home,
Amidst unfamiliar faces, a comforting grace,
A connection formed, in a fleeting embrace.

Through language barriers, our spirits entwine,
In the warmth of that smile, a moment divine,
A universal language, that knows no divide,
A stranger's smile, on this journey, a guide.

It speaks of kindness, of friendship's bloom,
In the midst of the unfamiliar, there's no gloom,
For in a simple gesture, a world is bridged,
A stranger's smile, where our souls are hitched.

In this vast tapestry of humanity's art,
A stranger's smile, a piece of the heart,
It reminds me that we're all one, hand in hand,
In the warmth of connection, across every land.

So let us carry with us, this lesson so worthwhile,
To share a piece of sunshine, with a stranger's smile,
For in these fleeting moments, we truly find,
The beauty of humanity, in hearts intertwined.

"Wanderlust's Fire" – The Passion that Drives Travelers

In the hearts of wanderers, there's a fire that burns,
An insatiable passion, a desire that yearns,
To explore the world, to chase the unknown,
In the depths of wanderlust, their spirits are sown.

It's the call of adventure, a relentless drive,
To journey to places where dreams come alive,
With each step they take, with each path they choose,
Wanderlust's fire, in their hearts, does infuse.

Through bustling cities and landscapes untamed,
In the beauty of diversity, they are named,
For in their travels, they find their true selves,
Wanderlust's fire, on their journey, propels.

It's the taste of new flavors, the scent of the breeze,
The embrace of foreign cultures, putting heart at ease,
With every new sunrise, they're reborn anew,
Wanderlust's fire, in their souls, it ensues.

Through the highs and lows of life's winding road,
In wanderlust's fire, their passions are stowed,
For the world's a playground, where dreams conspire,
In the hearts of wanderers, fueled by wanderlust's fire.

So let it burn bright, let it guide their way,
Wanderlust's fire, through night and through day,
For in their journeys, they find their greatest desire,
The flame of adventure, in wanderlust's fire.

"Seeker of Horizons" – The Constant Search for New Experiences

A seeker of horizons, I wander through the days,
In search of life's mysteries, in countless different ways,
With a heart that's open wide, and a curious mind,
I leave no stone unturned, no treasure left behind.

I chase the rising sun, in the early morning light,
To capture fleeting moments, in the day's first sight,
The world is my canvas, my dreams are my guide,
A seeker of horizons, with wanderlust as my pride.

Through forests thick with secrets, and mountains that soar,
I yearn to explore, to uncover, to implore,
The beauty of this world, in its every hidden nook,
A seeker of horizons, with an ever-open book.

I sail the open oceans, where the waters call,
To chart uncharted waters, to navigate them all,
With the wind in my hair, and the sea beneath my feet,
A seeker of horizons, where every voyage is a feat.

In bustling city streets, and in tranquil countryside,
I find stories untold, in every face and stride,
The tapestry of humanity, in each soul I meet,
A seeker of horizons, where cultures' rhythms beat.

Through laughter and through tears, in moments of delight,
I seek the threads of connection, in the day and the night,
For in the shared experiences, in the bonds that tie,
A seeker of horizons, I find life's reasons why.

With a backpack full of dreams, and a heart that's free,
I'll forever be a seeker, where the horizons meet me,
For in the constant journey, in the quest to explore,
A seeker of horizons, forever I'll soar.

"Journey Through Seasons" – The Changing Landscapes of Travel

In the canvas of travel, I trace the seasons' flow,
Each journey a chapter, in life's ebb and glow,
Through the spring's tender bloom, in nature's embrace,
I wander through blossoms, in a soft, fragrant space.

Summer's golden rays, on distant shores they gleam,
As I chase the sunsets, like an endless dream,
In the warmth of adventure, the world comes alive,
A symphony of colours, where moments thrive.

Autumn's leaves fall gently, in a poetic dance,
As I roam through forests, in nature's grand expanse,
The landscapes transform, in hues of amber and gold,
A journey through seasons, where stories are told.

Winter's icy breath, in the crisp, chilly air,
I trek through the snowfields, without a single care,
In the silence of snowfall, where the world turns to white,
A journey through seasons, in the soft, hushed night.

Through the cycles of life, I'll forever roam,
In the journey through seasons, I'll find my home,
For each chapter of travel, in its own special way,
Brings new perspectives, to cherish every day.

"Maps and Metaphors" – Finding Meaning in the Journey

In cartography's dance, maps unfold,
A journey's tale in lines of old.
Metaphors drawn on life's vast page,
Guiding hearts through every age.

Mountains rise, metaphors of might,
Challenges faced, reaching the height.
Rivers meander, a resilient stream,
Metaphors of strength in the sunbeam.

Cities stand as stories told,
Metaphors of dreams in streets of gold.
Oceans whisper metaphors profound,
Navigating depths, where truths are found.

Stars above, a celestial metaphor,
Guiding souls to a distant shore.
In the compass of dreams, our journey aligns,
Metaphors and maps, where meaning shines.

"Odyssey of Friendship" – Bonds Forged on the Road

In the Odyssey of Friendship, paths entwine,
As kindred spirits, in the tapestry of time.
On roads less traveled, where stories unfold,
Bonds are forged in adventures untold.

Through winding alleys and hills to climb,
Friendship blooms, an eternal paradigm.
Footprints on highways, beneath the open sky,
Laughter echoes, as the days pass by.

Side by side, facing storms and serene,
In the odyssey of friendship, a cherished scene.
Shared tales of triumphs, defeats laid bare,
In the warmth of companionship, none can compare.

Through the highs and lows, a steadfast guide,
Friendship's compass, in journeys far and wide.
Together we sail, through life's ebb and flow,
An odyssey of friendship, a bond that continues to grow.

In the tapestry of memories, woven and true,
Friendship's odyssey paints skies of azure hue.
With each step forward, hand in hand,
In the journey of friendship, we forever stand.

"Wandering Stars" – Celestial Navigation and Guidance

Beneath the canvas of the night, a celestial ballet,
Wandering stars, luminous guides, lighting the way.
Navigating realms unknown, their tales unfold,
In cosmic whispers and tales of silver and gold.

Orion's belt, a celestial sash in the velvet sky,
Wandering stars, like beacons, catch the eye.
With cosmic dust, they write their story,
Guiding seekers through the cosmic glory.

A cosmic ballet, the constellations' embrace,
Wandering stars, each a guide in grace.
In the silent dance of the Milky Way,
They chart a course, night and day.

Cassiopeia's throne, a celestial queen,
Wandering stars, on journeys unseen.
Through the vastness of the cosmic sea,
They guide with celestial synchronicity.

Oh, Polaris, steadfast in the northern night,
Wandering star, a navigator's delight.
In the vastness of the celestial dome,
They guide wanderers, calling them home.

Celestial navigation, a cosmic art,
Wandering stars, a map to every heart.
In the tapestry of the cosmic night,
They lead us to realms of pure starlight.

Follow these astral whispers, far and wide,
Wandering stars, forever our cosmic guide.
In the vast expanse where galaxies gleam,
Their celestial guidance is our eternal dream.

"The Open Road's Serenade" – Music and Travel Intertwined

On the open road's serenade, a symphony unfolds,
Tires humming a rhythm, as the journey molds.
Highways and melodies dance hand in hand,
Notes chasing horizons across the land.

Wind whispers secrets through the rolling song,
Asphalt and chords, where wanderers belong.
Guitars strumming stories of places yet untold,
The open road's serenade, an anthem bold.

Engine hums like a bass note in the night,
Traveling companions in harmonic flight.
Each bend and curve, a lyrical ride,
In the open road's serenade, emotions abide.

Tunes echo through canyons and city streets,
Traveling melodies where the heart beats.
The road and music, a timeless blend,
A serenade that journeys, never to end.

"Pilgrimage of Hope" – Seeking Solace and Inspiration on a Journey

In the pilgrimage of hope, I set my course,
Seeking solace in the world's boundless force,
With a heart open wide, and dreams as my guide,
I walk this sacred path, where faith and dreams collide.

Through rugged terrain, and under starry skies,
I seek the whispers of wisdom, where the old road lies,
In the footsteps of pilgrims, who've come before,
I find inspiration anew, in their stories and lore.

As I tread on this journey, both near and far,
I glimpse hope's eternal, like a distant star,
In the hearts of fellow travellers, we share the same scope,
In the pilgrimage of hope, we find solace and inspiration, our
constant trope.

With each step I take, I'm renewed and reborn,
In the pilgrimage of hope, where the soul is torn,
To pieces of beauty, and fragments of grace,
I find solace and inspiration, in this sacred space.

"Wanderer's Lullaby" – The Comfort of being on the Move

In the cradle of adventure, I softly sway,
A wanderer's lullaby, as I wander each day,
The road is my lullaby, the stars overhead,
A blanket of dreams, where I lay my head.

I find comfort in motion, as I journey along,
With each step I take, I find where I belong,
The world is my cradle, its rhythms, my guide,
A wanderer's lullaby, on this path I'll reside.

Through valleys and mountains, by rivers that flow,
In the whisper of breezes, I find peace in the go,
The horizon's my melody, it sings without cease,
A wanderer's lullaby, my heart finds release.

Underneath the open sky, I restlessly roam,
A wanderer's lullaby, it calls me to roam,
In the arms of the unknown, I quietly sigh,
For the comfort of movement, beneath the same sky.

"Destinations of the Mind" – The Power of Visualization in Travel

In the vast landscapes of my mind, I roam,
Creating destinations, a world of my own,
With closed eyes, I visualize the places to find,
The power of imagination, in travel confined.

I sail on dreams' seas to islands afar,
Underneath the moon, beneath every star,
In my mind's eye, I explore without end,
Destinations created, around each bend.

I climb mountains of thought, reaching heights so grand,
Walking through memories, in the mind's endless land,
In the theatre of my thoughts, adventures unwind,
Destinations of the mind, uniquely designed.

With a canvas of colours, my mind paints the way,
Creating new landscapes, both night and day,
In the boundless realms of thoughts undefined,
I find endless travel, in destinations of the mind.

"Voyage to Inner Worlds" – Exploring the Depths of One's Soul

A voyage to inner worlds, where shadows reside,
In the chambers of the heart, where secrets hide,
I set sail on a journey, no compass or chart,
To explore the depths within, where emotions impart.

Through the labyrinth of memories, I gently tread,
In the echoes of pasts, where emotions have bled,
I uncover the layers, the stories untold,
In the voyage to inner worlds, where mysteries unfold.

In the caverns of solitude, I seek to understand,
The essence of my being, the grains of sand,
I delve into the darkness, where fears may abide,
In the voyage to inner worlds, I let go of my pride.

Through the rivers of tears, and the storms of despair,
I navigate with courage, with hope in the air,
In the mirror of reflection, I see my true face,
In the voyage to inner worlds, I find my own grace.

With each step inward, I find strength anew,
In the voyage to inner worlds, I discover what's true,
For the greatest journey of all, it's often opined,
Is the voyage to inner worlds, the soul's quest defined.

"Rhymes of the Road" – The Poetry Found in Everyday Travels

In the rhythm of wheels on the asphalt's grace,
Rhymes of the road, in every journey's embrace,
Each mile a stanza, each turn a refrain,
In the poetry of travel, we find life's sweet gain.

The highway's verses, the whispers of the breeze,
Through open windows, they dance with such ease,
The road signs and billboards, the stories they share,
In the rhymes of the road, we're always aware.

The engine's cadence, a steady beat,
As we traverse the world, from street to street,
In the hum of the tires, the songs of the car,
Rhymes of the road, no matter how far.

The landscapes we pass, each a vivid line,
In nature's poetry, forever entwined,
In the journeys we make, both near and abroad,
In the rhymes of the road, we find life's sweet reward.

"Adventures in Solitude" – Finding Peace in Being Alone on the Road

In the solitude of the road, I find my way,
Adventures in solitude, where peace holds sway,
The world outside fades, as I journey alone,
In the quiet of my thoughts, my spirit is sown.

Beneath the endless sky, I tread the unknown,
Adventures in solitude, my heart's cornerstone,
With each step I take, the worries take flight,
In the stillness of the road, my soul takes its flight.

Through whispering forests and along silent streams,
Adventures in solitude, where solitude gleams,
I'm not lonely, for I've found solace in me,
In the embrace of the road, I am forever free.

With only the wind as my trusted guide,
Adventures in solitude, where fears subside,
I commune with nature, with stars that shine bright,
In the vastness of the world, I find pure delight.

In the embrace of silence, I hear my own song,
Adventures in solitude, where I truly belong,
For in being alone, I've discovered life's grace,
In the adventures of solitude, I've found my own place.

"Wandering Hearts" – Love Stories Set Against Different Landscapes

In lands where the mountains kiss the sky so high,
Two wandering hearts met beneath the sun's soft sigh,
Their love story painted on a canvas so vast,
In the rugged terrain, where their love was cast.

Beside the ocean's waves, where the seagulls soar,
Two wandering hearts found love on the shore,
Their love like the tides, ebbing and flowing,
In the whispers of the sea breeze, their love kept growing.

In the heart of the city, where the lights burn bright,
Two wandering hearts danced through the night,
Their love story unfolded in the urban embrace,
In the bustling streets, where they found their place.

Amidst the quiet meadows, where wildflowers bloom,
Two wandering hearts found love in nature's room,
Their love like the breeze, gentle and free,
In the serenity of the fields, where their love would be.

In ancient ruins, where history whispers its tale,
Two wandering hearts found love in a past's detail,
Their love story etched in the stones so old,
In the echoes of time, their love was bold.

On a journey together, their love knows no bounds,
Two wandering hearts, in each other, they've found,
In landscapes diverse, their love story unfurls,
For wandering hearts, love is the greatest of pearls.

"Journey to Tranquillity" – Seeking Peace and Serenity Through Travel

On a journey to tranquility, I set my sails,
Seeking peace and serenity in distant trails,
Through valleys and mountains, and rivers that glide,
I yearn for the solace, where my heart will reside.

Beneath the open sky, I find my sanctuary,
In the whispers of nature, my heart finds its key,
The rustling leaves, the gentle, calming streams,
In the journey to tranquility, I chase my dreams.

In ancient forests, where time stands still,
I seek the hush of serenity, a tranquil thrill,
With each step I take, I leave behind the fray,
In the journey to tranquility, I find my way.

Amidst rolling hills, where wildflowers bloom,
I find solace in the quiet, in nature's room,
In the embrace of silence, where my soul takes flight,
In the journey to tranquility, I find my inner light.

As the world whirls on, I seek my reprieve,
In the journey to tranquility, I choose to believe,
That amid life's chaos, in the midst of the strife,
I'll find peace and serenity, in the tapestry of life.

"Verse of the Voyager" – The Poet's Perspective on Journeys

In the verse of the voyager, I weave my tales,
Of journeys embarked, and distant trails,
With pen in hand, and heart as my guide,
I paint the landscapes where my soul does ride.

Through mountains and valleys, and skies so wide,
I seek the stories that in travels reside,
In the footsteps of travelers, I find my muse,
In the verse of the voyager, my spirit does fuse.

I wander through cities, where cultures entwine,
In the bustling streets, I find stories divine,
With every encounter, a verse comes to be,
In the verse of the voyager, I set my words free.

I sail the open seas, where the horizons unfold,
In the tales of the ocean, my stories are told,
With each wave that crashes, with each ship that sails,
In the verse of the voyager, my passion prevails.

Through deserts of sand, where the winds do play,
In the arid landscapes, I find my own way,
In the silence of solitude, a verse takes its form,
In the verse of the voyager, my heart finds its norm.

In the tapestry of travel, my verses are spun,
In the heart of the wanderer, they are second to none,
For in every journey, a new tale to discover,
In the verse of the voyager, I am an eternal lover.

"Whispers of Wisdom" – Lessons Learned from the Road

In the whispers of wisdom, the road unfolds,
Lessons learned in journeys, in stories untold,
As I wander through life, in its ebb and its flow,
The road whispers secrets, in its gentle, hushed glow.

Through mountains and valleys, in the wilderness vast,
Whispers of wisdom, in each moment I'm cast,
The trials and triumphs, the joys and the strife,
In the whispers of wisdom, I sculpt my own life.

In the footsteps of others, whose paths I've crossed,
Whispers of wisdom, in memories embossed,
Their stories, their laughter, their sorrows, their grace,
In the whispers of wisdom, I find my own place.

Beneath the open sky, where the stars brightly gleam,
Whispers of wisdom, like a beautiful dream,
The constellations above, with their tales in the night,
In the whispers of wisdom, I find my own light.

In the cities I've roamed, where cultures unite,
Whispers of wisdom, in every street's light,
The diversity of voices, the harmony in the sound,
In the whispers of wisdom, my perspectives are bound.

Through the pages of time, where history's ink flows,
Whispers of wisdom, in the stories it shows,
The rise and the fall, the empires that stand,
In the whispers of wisdom, I grasp life's grand plan.

In the embrace of nature, where serenity thrives,
Whispers of wisdom, in the wind and the hives,
The cycles of seasons, the river's soft stream,
In the whispers of wisdom, I discover life's theme.

Through moments of silence, in reflection I find,
Whispers of wisdom, in the quiet of mind,
The answers within, where the heart takes its cue,
In the whispers of wisdom, I find what is true.

So, in this journey of life, with its stories to come,
Whispers of wisdom, I'll forever become,
For the road is my teacher, with lessons untold,
In the whispers of wisdom, my spirit takes hold.

"Ode to the Explorer" – Honouring those who Seek the Unknown

Ode to the explorer, with courage in your heart,
You sail uncharted waters, where adventures start,
Through dense and silent forests, where secrets hide,
You dare to tread where few have dared, side by side.

In the heart of the desert, where the sun beats down,
You march with steadfast purpose, on endless ground,
Over towering mountains, you climb with zeal,
Ode to the explorer, your spirit is real.

With stars as your compass, you chart the night sky,
In the depths of the oceans, where mysteries lie,
Through bustling city streets, and alleys unknown,
You seek the stories, where humanity's sown.

Ode to the explorer, your quest is your guide,
In the journeys you make, where the world opens wide,
You teach us the lessons of courage and grace,
As you venture forth, finding your own place.

In the embrace of nature, where wild places dwell,
You find solace and wonder, in every tale to tell,
Through adversity and triumph, your spirit's made strong,
Ode to the explorer, we sing your song.

So here's to the wanderers, the seekers, the free,
Ode to the explorer, in you, we all see,
The unquenchable fire, the spirit untamed,
In your journeys, our world is forever named.

"Wanderlust's Legacy" – Passing Down the Love of Travel Through Generations

In the heart of wanderlust's legacy, we find,
A timeless passion passed, from one to another's mind,
Through tales of distant shores, and adventures untold,
The love of travel's fire, from young to old.

In the stories we share, around the fireside's glow,
Wanderlust's legacy, in each tale does grow,
From grandparent to parent, from child to child,
The wanderer's spirit, forever beguiled.

With maps and compasses, we learn to explore,
In the wanderlust's legacy, our spirits do implore,
To seek the horizons, to journey afar,
To follow in the footsteps of those who've been our star.

So, we pass down the love of travel, hand to hand,
In wanderlust's legacy, our spirits understand,
That the world's a vast canvas, for us to explore,
To keep the flames of wanderlust forevermore.

"Tracks of Timelessness" – Moments that Transcend Time During a Journey

In the tracks of timelessness, moments unfold,
During a journey, where stories are told,
Through ancient pathways and modern trails,
We find moments that transcend time's veils.

In a medieval town, where cobblestones guide,
Tracks of timelessness, in the streets we stride,
The echoes of history, in the stones they reside,
In the heart of the past, our souls are tied.

On a train through landscapes, both wild and serene,
Tracks of timelessness, in each passing scene,
As the world rushes by, in a rhythmic rhyme,
We glimpse eternity, in fleeting time.

In a forest's embrace, where the ancient trees stand,
Tracks of timelessness, in the shadows they expand,
The whispers of nature, a timeless refrain,
In the midst of the woods, we find solace again.

By the shores of the sea, where the waves kiss the shore,
Tracks of timelessness, in the ocean's grandeur,
As the tides ebb and flow, in a ceaseless ballet,
We touch eternity, in the endless waves' display.

In a bustling city square, where life's colors blend,
Tracks of timelessness, in the stories they send,
In the laughter and chatter, and the moments we share,
We find the eternal, in the bonds we wear.

In the stillness of a canyon, where the echoes resound,
Tracks of timelessness, in the silence profound,
As the wind whispers secrets, in the rock's ancient rhyme,
We hear eternity, in the canyon's timeless chime.

Through moments that linger, and memories that last,
Tracks of timelessness, in the moments that pass,
In journeys we embark on, both near and so far,
We discover the timeless, in moments where we are.

For in the tracks of timelessness, our spirits align,
Moments that transcend time, in the tapestry of time.

"Voyage to Tomorrow" – The Anticipation of Future Travels

In the soft light of dawn, where dreams take their flight,
Voyage to tomorrow, in the morning's first light,
Anticipation blooms like a flower in May,
As I set my course for adventures on my way.

In the maps yet uncharted, in the roads yet untrod,
Voyage to tomorrow, where the world seems so broad,
With each step that I take, and each mile on the track,
I anticipate the journeys, that there's no looking back.

The cities unexplored, where cultures entwine,
Voyage to tomorrow, in each vibrant design,
In the cuisine and the stories, the laughter and the song,
Anticipation grows, as I journey along.

Through valleys and mountains, and by rivers that stream,
Voyage to tomorrow, in landscapes that gleam,
In the wilderness' embrace, where nature runs wild,
Anticipation dances, like a carefree child.

As I look to the future, with wonder and glee,
Voyage to tomorrow, in the world yet to be,
In the journeys that await, with each dawn's new glow,
Anticipation guides me, as I continue to grow.

So, I set my sails high, with a heart that is free,
Voyage to tomorrow, where my spirit finds glee,
In the thrill of the unknown, where the path leads the way,
Anticipation fills me, as I venture each day.

"Wandering Souls" – The Idea that Some are Born to Wander

In the tapestry of life, where destinies entwine,
There are those born to wander, beneath the starry sign,
Their souls are nomadic, like the restless breeze,
In the world's grand theater, they seek to find their ease.

With each dawn's awakening, they hear the road's sweet call,
Wandering souls, they're bound to roam, to explore, to enthral,
They wander through the meadows, through cities far and wide,
In the embrace of nature, or where cultures coincide.

Through deserts' arid sands, and mountains that scrape the sky,
Wandering souls, they seek the heights, they're born to fly,
In the rhythm of the journey, where paths are undefined,
They find their truest purpose, in the stories intertwined.

Through the pages of history, their footprints lightly tread,
Wandering souls, their tales are told, both in heart and head,
They leave behind a legacy, in the places they have been,
In the hearts of fellow travelers, in the places they have seen.

They're the dreamers and the wanderers, the seekers of the new,
Wandering souls, they're fueled by dreams, in all they pursue,
With hearts full of adventure, and eyes that sparkle bright,
They journey through life's wonders, beneath the day and night.

In the quiet of solitude, or where crowds may swarm,
Wandering souls, they find their peace, in the endless form,
For in their restless spirits, in the paths they dare to tread,
We find the wanderlust's fire, forever burning red.

So here's to the wanderers, those born to roam and roam,
Wandering souls, in their journeys, they find home,
In the vast expanse of the world, where their stories unfurl,
They teach us the beauty of wandering, in this grand,
precious whirl.

"Journey to Gratitude" – Appreciating the Beauty of the World

In the journey to gratitude, we open our eyes,
To the world's wondrous beauty, beneath the open skies,
With every step we take, and every breath we breathe,
We find reasons to be thankful, in what we can perceive.

In the dawn's first light, where the sun paints the morn,
Journey to gratitude, in the day being born,
In the colors that mingle, in the horizon's embrace,
We find gratitude's presence, in nature's lovely grace.

In the laughter of children, in their innocent glee,
Journey to gratitude, in their spirits so free,
In the hope they inspire, and the love they impart,
We find gratitude's essence, in the depths of our heart.

In the kindness of strangers, in the warmth of a smile,
Journey to gratitude, even for a little while,
In the gestures of compassion, in humanity's art,
We find gratitude's magic, in every beating heart.

In the quiet of evening, as the stars softly gleam,
Journey to gratitude, in the night's gentle dream,
In the peace that surrounds us, in the calm of the night,
We find gratitude's solace, in the soft, gentle light.

In the embrace of loved ones, in the bonds that we share,
Journey to gratitude, in the love that's so rare,
In the connections we treasure, in the moments we hold,
We find gratitude's treasure, more precious than gold.

So let us journey to gratitude, with hearts open wide,
Appreciating the beauty of the world, far and wide,
In the tapestry of life, in each moment we meet,
We find gratitude's symphony, in every heartbeat.

"Rhymes of Resilience" – Overcoming Challenges on the Road

In the rhymes of resilience, our stories are spun,
Tales of overcoming, of battles hard-won,
As we journey through life, on paths unforeseen,
In the face of challenges, we find what we mean.

Through the stormy seas, where the tempests rage,
Rhymes of resilience, we turn a new page,
With courage as our compass, we sail through the night,
In the darkest of waters, we still seek the light.

In the heart of the wilderness, where dangers may lurk,
Rhymes of resilience, in the wild we must work,
With determination unyielding, we tread the unknown,
In the face of adversity, our strength is our own.

On the steep mountain slopes, where the air grows thin,
Rhymes of resilience, in each step, we begin,
To conquer the summits, where dreams touch the sky,
In the face of obstacles, we reach ever high.

In the bustling city streets, where chaos does reign,
Rhymes of resilience, through every strain,
With perseverance unbroken, we forge our own way,
In the urban jungles, we thrive every day.

Through the trials we face, both great and small,
Rhymes of resilience, in us, they enthrall,
For it's in overcoming, we find our true grace,
In the rhymes of resilience, life's challenges we embrace.

In the stories we tell, in the journeys we share,
Rhymes of resilience, in the trials, we declare,
That no matter the obstacle, the road, or the mile,
In the rhymes of resilience, we find our own style.

"Adventures in Wonder" – Embracing the Awe-Inspiring Aspects of Travel

In adventures of wonder, I find my delight,
Embracing the awe, in the day and the night,
As I journey through landscapes, so vast and so grand,
In the wonders of travel, I take a firm stand.

Beneath star-studded skies, where galaxies twirl,
Adventures in wonder, like a magical whirl,
In the cosmos above, where mysteries unfold,
In the awe of the universe, my spirit is bold.

Through forests that whisper, with secrets untold,
Adventures in wonder, in nature's stronghold,
In the rustling leaves, and the songs of the breeze,
In the wonder of creation, my soul finds its ease.

On the shores of the ocean, where waves kiss the land,
Adventures in wonder, in the endless sand,
In the rhythm of tides, and the seagull's cry,
In the vastness of horizons, my dreams reach the sky.

In the cities of wonder, where cultures unite,
Adventures in wonder, in the city's own light,
In the diversity of voices, and the stories they bear,
In the wonder of humanity, I find love in the air.

In adventures of wonder, my heart takes its flight,
Embracing the awe, in the day and the night,
For in every journey, a marvel I find,
In the wonders of travel, I'm forever entwined.

⎯⎯⎯⎯⎯✴⎯⎯⎯⎯⎯

"Wandering Echoes" – Remembering the Stories of those Met on the Road

Wandering echoes of voices once near,
In the journeys we've shared, in moments so dear,
Their stories still linger, like whispers in air,
In the tapestry of memory, they're always there.

On the road we've crossed paths, in distant terrains,
In the laughter and tears, in joy and in pains,
Their tales were a gift, in our hearts they reside,
Wandering echoes of souls, forever our guide.

Though time may have passed, and distances spread,
In the wandering echoes, our spirits are wed,
For the stories we've gathered, like treasures they gleam,
Wandering echoes, in our hearts, a cherished dream.

"Pathways of Purpose" – Finding Meaning in One's Journey

On the pathways of purpose, I tread with intent,
Seeking meaning in my journey, where my spirit is sent,
Through the twists and the turns, in the road's winding grace,
I find purpose in each step, in each moment's embrace.

In the bonds that I forge, with kindred souls I meet,
Pathways of purpose, where connection is sweet,
In the friendships that blossom, in love that's revealed,
I discover the meaning, in hearts that are healed.

Through challenges faced, in the trials I endure,
Pathways of purpose, in the lessons so pure,
In the strength that I gather, in the wisdom I gain,
I discern my life's purpose, in the midst of the pain.

In the beauty of nature, in the world's grand design,
Pathways of purpose, in the moments that shine,
In the sunrise's splendor, in the starry night's grace,
I uncover my purpose, in this vast, boundless space.

In the act of creation, in the work of my hand,
Pathways of purpose, where my dreams take their stand,
In the passion I harbor, in each goal I pursue,
I find meaning and purpose, in the things that I do.

Through the laughter and tears, through the joy and the strife,
Pathways of purpose, in the tapestry of life,
In the story unfolding, in each chapter's embrace,
I find purpose and meaning, in this exquisite chase.

So, on the pathways of purpose, I journey each day,
Seeking meaning and purpose, in every which way,
In the dance of existence, in the song of my soul,
I find my life's purpose, where my heart finds its goal.

"Odyssey of Belonging" – Exploring One's Sense of Place in the World

In the odyssey of belonging, I take my stride,
Exploring the world's tapestry, far and wide,
Through bustling cities and tranquil, open lands,
I search for the place where my heart truly stands.

In the midst of diverse cultures, where voices blend,
Odyssey of belonging, in the friendships we rend,
In shared laughter and stories, the bonds that we weave,
I seek a sense of place in the hearts that believe.

Amidst nature's wonders, where wild spirits roam,
Odyssey of belonging, in the wilderness's home,
In the whispering leaves and the rivers that flow,
I yearn to uncover where my spirit can grow.

In the roots of my heritage, where my lineage began,
Odyssey of belonging, in the steps of each clan,
In the warmth of my home, with loved ones so dear,
I discover the essence of where I truly adhere.

So, on this grand odyssey, I continue to roam,
Exploring the world to find where I belong,
In the tapestry of life, where the journey's unfurled,
Odyssey of belonging, in this vast, wondrous world.

"Wanderer's Journal" – Recording Thoughts and Memories on the Road

In the wanderer's journal, pages worn and old,
I record the tales and memories, in stories yet untold,
Through cities and deserts, mountains tall and wide,
I pen the essence of my journey, where my heart takes its ride.

In the ink of my thoughts, I etch each passing sight,
Wanderer's journal, in day and in night,
In the faces I meet, in their laughter and their tears,
I write the chapters of my travel, throughout the years.

Beneath the open sky, where the stars brightly gleam,
In the wanderer's journal, I capture every dream,
In the quiet of nature, where the wilderness thrives,
I describe the wonders I've witnessed, in my life's archives.

By the shores of the sea, where the waves kiss the land,
Wanderer's journal, in the soft, shifting sand,
In the rhythm of the tides, and the seagull's cry,
I narrate the stories of my journeys, reaching for the sky.

In the bustling city streets, where cultures unite,
In the wanderer's journal, each moment takes flight,
In the diversity of voices, in the tapestry of life,
I chronicle the experiences, in this grand, worldly strife.

Through the seasons of life, in the tapestry of time,
Wanderer's journal, each verse, each rhyme,
In the laughter and tears, in joy and in despair,
I write the verses of my odyssey, everywhere.

So, as I wander and roam, where my footsteps may trod,
In the wanderer's journal, I find a connection with God,
In the written and unwritten, in the stories I collect,
I carry the wanderer's journal, where my soul reflects.

"Tracks of Transformation" – How Travel Changes us

In the tapestry of time, where destinies align,
Tracks of transformation, etched in every line.
Journey's rhythmic cadence, a dance with the unknown,
Through landscapes of the heart, our evolution's sown.

The train of life departs, from the station of our birth,
On tracks unseen, we navigate our dreams and worth.
Each whistle's echo whispers tales of the sublime,
A metamorphic pilgrimage, transcending space and time.

At dawn, we board with hope, the carriages of chance,
Bound for realms unseen, in a cosmic dance.
Through valleys of despair and peaks of pure elation,
We find ourselves remade in the alchemy of navigation.

The click-clack symphony, a song of ceaseless change,
As scenery unfolds, perspectives rearrange.
The windows frame reflections of the soul's progression,
As we traverse the terrains of self-discovery's confession.

Along the tracks, encounters with the fleeting now,
Kindred spirits, lessons, etchings on the brow.
In each fleeting station, a chance to leave behind,
The baggage of the past, the burdens of the mind.

Mountains stand as mentors, rivers preach in flow,
Deserts teach resilience, the winds in wisdom blow.
Underneath the canvas of the ever-shifting sky,
We metamorphose, as the old selves bid goodbye.

The tracks bear witness to the stories we unfold,
Of resilience and triumph, of the young and old.
As wheels hum a ballad of the journeys we've embraced,
We emerge transformed, in the travel's sacred grace.

For in the act of moving, we become the change,
Embracing the unknown, in destinies arranged.
Tracks of transformation, stretching far and wide,
A testament to the magic of the journey's tide.

"Inkwell Odyssey" – The Writer's Perspective on Journeys

In the inkwell's deep abyss, an odyssey unfolds,
A writer's journey, where tales and dreams are told.
Quill sails on parchment seas, words a compass true,
Navigating realms untold, where creativity brews.

Through stanzas and verses, the expedition begins,
In the labyrinth of thoughts, where inspiration wins.
Metaphors and similes, like constellations align,
An odyssey in every sentence, a universe in each line.

Ink-stained fingers map the landscapes of the mind,
Crafting narratives, a voyage uniquely designed.
Characters embark on quests, emotions ebb and flow,
In the inkwell odyssey, imagination's currents grow.

The poet's ship sails on the waves of metaphor,
Exploring the depths of language, seeking evermore.
In the parchment vastness, where ideas converge,
A writer's odyssey, an eternal surge.

As quill kisses paper, stories come to life,
A symphony of words, a ballet of endless strife.
In the inkwell's odyssey, where creation takes flight,
The writer's journey, an everlasting night.

"Journey to the Unknown" – Facing the Fear of the Unfamiliar

Beneath the cloak of twilight, a journey unfolds,
To the unknown realms where mystery molds.
Footprints in uncertainty, fear's chilling embrace,
Yet courage kindles, a flicker in the vastness of space.

A path veiled in shadows, whispers of the unseen,
A symphony of doubts, where courage intervenes.
Through the thickets of anxiety, a traveler strides,
Facing the fear of the unknown, where darkness resides.

Moonlight becomes a guide, painting silhouettes bold,
The heart's lantern flickers, a story to be told.
In the tapestry of uncertainty, threads of resolve,
A journey to the unknown, where fears dissolve.

Horizons beckon with enigma, a canvas unexplored,
Yet in each step forward, courage is restored.
The compass of curiosity points to uncharted lands,
As the traveler discovers, fear slowly disbands.

Bridges of bravery span the rivers of doubt,
Echoes of footsteps drown the fear's own shout.
In the vast expanse where shadows dance and play,
The journey to the unknown becomes the traveler's way.

Embracing the ambiguity, like a cloak worn with pride,
The voyage unfolds, with fear cast aside.
For in the heart's wilderness, where courage is sown,
We find strength anew in the journey unknown.

"Verse of Exploration" – Poetry as a Means of Discovery

In the verses, I embark on a quest,
Exploring realms within, where emotions nest.
Stanzas unfold like uncharted terrain,
A poetic odyssey, free from the mundane.

Metaphors blossom, a language untold,
In the verse of exploration, secrets unfold.
Rhymes echo like footsteps on unexplored ground,
A journey of self in the poetic surround.

Lines intertwine, weaving tales to find,
The uncharted landscapes of the creative mind.
In each syllable, a discovery's birth,
The verse of exploration, the poet's rebirth.

"Trail of Endurance" – Perseverance in the Face of Challenges During Travel

On the trail of endurance, where the journey unfolds,
Beneath skies of challenge, and tales yet to be told.
Mountains rise like obstacles, their peaks sublime,
Yet each rocky ascent, a testament to time.

Rivers of adversity may attempt to detain,
But the trail of endurance persists through the strain.
Through valleys of shadows, where doubt may accrue,
Each step a declaration that courage will renew.

Storms may unleash torrents, and winds may assail,
Yet the traveler presses on, determination set sail.
In the crucible of trials, where hardships may enthrall,
The trail of endurance becomes a testament to all.

Footprints etch resilience on the path's rugged face,
A narrative of tenacity, a testament to grace.
In the quietude of struggle, where echoes persist,
Endurance is a melody, a harmonious twist.

Through the labyrinth of challenges, the heart finds its tune,
A symphony of resilience, played under the moon.
For in every step taken, on this arduous course,
The trail of endurance becomes a relentless force.

And when the horizon fades into the twilight's blend,
A weary traveler finds strength in the bends.
For the journey persists, an unwavering dance,
On the enduring trail, where hope and courage enhance.

"Voyaging Through Verses" – Poetic Reflections on a Journey

Voyaging through verses, a poetic expedition,
Navigating stanzas, an introspective mission.
In the sea of words, where emotions ebb and flow,
A journey unfolds, in the poet's ebb and tow.

Lines on the page, like a trail of breadcrumbs,
Leading through metaphors, where imagination succumbs.
In the cadence of rhyme, echoes of footsteps resound,
On this lyrical journey, where meanings are found.

Through valleys of metaphor and peaks of inspiration,
The poet explores realms, a boundless exploration.
Each stanza, a port of call in the vast expanse,
Where the pen charts courses, and thoughts dance.

Moonlit sonnets illuminate the poet's way,
Guided by constellations in the creative array.
Voyaging through verses, the heart's silent converse,
A poetic pilgrimage, where sentiments immerse.

In the tapestry of language, emotions are spun,
A journey through verses, a tale yet begun.
As the poet sails through the ink-stained sea,
Voyaging through verses, forever wild and free.

"Rhymes of Renewal" – Finding New Energy and Purpose Through Travel

In the verses of dawn, where sunlight gently streams,
Rhymes of renewal awaken dormant dreams.
Embarking on a journey, a pilgrimage of the soul,
Traveling to places where new energies unroll.

Mountains whisper secrets, rejuvenating the spirit,
As footsteps echo, a renewal is implicit.
Each sunrise paints the canvas of a day reborn,
In the symphony of travel, a melody is sworn.

Seas whisper tales of resilience and change,
On the shores of renewal, where destinies arrange.
The wind carries whispers of a purpose yet untold,
In the rhymes of renewal, a story unfolds.

Cities pulse with vibrant energies anew,
As travelers embrace a horizon so true.
Through the alleys of discovery, purpose is found,
In the rhymes of renewal, where hearts are unbound.

"Whispers of the Wanderer" – Secrets Shared Between Travelers

In the twilight's hush, where shadows softly play,
Whispers of the wanderer weave tales of the day.
Shared secrets linger in the air like a gentle breeze,
Between kindred souls, beneath ancient trees.

Footprints trace stories on paths worn and wide,
As the wanderer's heart unveils tales from inside.
In the quietude of campfires, by the river's side,
Whispers exchanged, in the traveler's confide.

Mountains stand witness, their peaks touching the sky,
As the wanderer's tales ascend, a soaring high.
Moonlit conversations, under the canvas of stars,
Echoing the wanderer's dreams that travel far.

Through the meandering roads and open fields,
Whispers of the wanderer, where authenticity yields.
In shared glances and unspoken words, they find,
A language universal, between hearts aligned.

———— ❈ ————

"Wanderlust's Rhapsody" – The Musicality of the Open Road

In the wanderlust's rhapsody, the open road's refrain,
A symphony of tires humming, an anthem without chain.
Asphalt becomes the sheet music, the horizon a grand score,
Tires dance in rhythm, on landscapes to explore.

The engine's purr, a bass note low and deep,
Wind's gentle whistle, a melody to keep.
Highways stretch like verses, in a poetic rhyme,
Underneath the canvas of the boundless time.

In the crescendo of mountains, where echoes play,
Wanderlust's rhapsody unfolds in a serenade array.
Fields and meadows join the chorus, their voices bright,
As the road unwinds, weaving day into night.

Each curve and bend, a musical transition,
The road, a ballad of perpetual audition.
Bridges hum a harmony, rivers contribute a song,
Wanderlust's rhapsody, a journey lifelong.

Through the cadence of travel, a story's melody told,
Wanderlust's rhapsody, an adventure to behold.
The tires' staccato, a heartbeat on the roam,
In the open road's sonnet, the wanderer finds home.

"Trails of Reflection" – Moments of Introspection During a Journey

On trails of reflection, where footsteps softly tread,
Moments of introspection, like whispers in my head.
Through winding pathways, beneath a contemplative sky,
The journey unfolds, and the soul begins to pry.

Mountains stand as mentors, guardians of the quiet,
As shadows play in valleys, where thoughts ignite.
In the hush of nature, a symphony of calm,
Trails of reflection weave an introspective psalm.

Each step becomes a question, every pause a reply,
The trail of introspection, under the vast, open sky.
Rivers mirror ponderings, flowing thoughts downstream,
On trails of reflection, where introspections gleam.

The rustle of leaves, a gentle confidante,
As the trail winds onward, in silent enchant.
Beneath the canopy, where sunlight filters through,
Trails of reflection illuminate the path anew.

In the quiet corners of the journey's introspective maze,
Contours of self-discovery emerge in myriad ways.
On trails of reflection, where echoes find connection,
The traveler discovers the art of introspection.

"Quest for Connection" – Seeking Common Ground with Diverse Cultures

In the quest for connection, across cultures we roam,
A journey to bridge, to make distant lands feel like home.
Through languages diverse, and customs rich and grand,
Seeking common ground, where understanding may stand.

In bazaars bustling, and on streets unknown,
The quest for connection, like seeds subtly sown.
Eyes meet, transcending borders, and smiles bloom,
Uniting hearts in a dance, erasing cultural gloom.

Through spices' allure, and tales untold,
The quest for connection, a human story to unfold.
In shared laughter and music's embrace,
Differences dissolve, leaving only grace.

A global tapestry woven with threads so fine,
The quest for connection, a universal design.
In the symphony of cultures, a harmonious sound,
The world's unity, in connection, is found.

"Adventures in Elegance" – Beauty Encountered During Travel

In adventures draped in elegance, where beauty takes its cue,
Nature paints masterpieces, skies of azure blue.
Mountains stand as sculptures, majestically defined,
Their silhouettes in sunset, a gallery enshrined.

City lights sparkle, a dance of urban grace,
In the night's soft glow, a cosmopolitan embrace.
Seas whisper serenades along the sandy shore,
Adventures in elegance, where wonders adore.

Cobbled streets echo stories of history's romance,
In ancient cities, each step's a subtle dance.
Sunflowers bow to the sun in golden exuberance,
Adventures in elegance, a traveler's dalliance.

"Wandering Poet's Dream" – The Ideal Journey from a Poet's Perspective

In the wandering poet's dream, a realm unfurled,
Where verses bloom like flowers in a poetic world.
Mountains echo sonnets, their peaks in rhyme,
As the poet traverses landscapes, unfettered by time.

Rivers weave ballads, flowing with melodic grace,
Whispers of the breeze, a gentle embrace.
Underneath a starlit canvas, tales unfold,
In the wandering poet's dream, a story untold.

Each step a stanza, every pause a refrain,
The ideal journey, a poet's sweetest gain.
Fields of inspiration, where thoughts gently gleam,
In the wandering poet's dream, reality's supreme.

Cities pulse with rhythms, a metropolis in verse,
Streets alive with lyrics, a melodic converse.
In this poetic odyssey, where imagination is the theme,
The wandering poet dreams, in a world agleam.

"Pathways to Discovery" – The Journey as a Process of Self-Discovery

On pathways to discovery, where the horizon meets the soul,
Footprints trace tales of a journey, a narrative to unroll.
Through verdant meadows and deserts wide,
The traveler embarks on a quest, with self as the guide.

Mountains stand as mentors, whispering ancient lore,
As rivers carve paths, reflecting the explorer.
Beneath the open canvas of the ever-changing sky,
Self-discovery unfolds, where old selves bid goodbye.

Each twist and turn, a chapter unfurls,
In the book of self, where the heart whirls.
The echoes of footsteps, a rhythmic conversation,
On pathways to discovery, a symphony of revelation.

In the silence of solitude, and the chaos of the crowd,
The journey becomes a mirror, both quiet and loud.
Through the labyrinth of time, where the self weaves,
Pathways to discovery lead to the essence one retrieves.

"Odyssey of Imagination" – The Limitless Potential of the Mind During Travel

In the odyssey of imagination, the mind takes flight,
A boundless journey, where dreams alight.
Through landscapes of thought, uncharted and vast,
The traveler within explores realms that last.

Mountains of creativity touch the canvas of the mind,
As the odyssey unfolds, endless possibilities find.
Rivers of inspiration carve paths unexplored,
In the realm of imagination, where visions are stored.

Skies of wonder stretch with limitless hue,
The odyssey of imagination paints horizons anew.
Footprints echo in the corridors of thought,
As the mind roams freely, unbridled and sought.

In this odyssey, the poet's pen takes charge,
Scripting tales untold, on the imagination's barge.
The traveler within, guided by dreams' elation,
Embarks on an odyssey of boundless imagination.

"Wanderer's Waltz" – Dance and Movement as Metaphors for Travel

In the wanderer's waltz, on the dance floor of the earth,
Footsteps paint stories, tales of wanderlust's birth.
Mountains are partners, in a rhythmic embrace,
As the wanderer twirls, exploring grace.

Through meadows, a pirouette in the golden light,
In the wanderer's waltz, where day turns into night.
Rivers join the rhythm, a flowing ballet,
As the wanderer follows the choreography of the day.

City streets become a tango, with lights as partners,
The wanderer's waltz, a dance that never falters.
Each step, a journey, each turn, a new chance,
In the wanderer's waltz, the world does a dance.

Underneath the canopy of stars, a celestial ball,
The wanderer's waltz, in moonlight's thrall.
Through the choreography of landscapes vast,
The wanderer's waltz is a journey unsurpassed.

In the dance of travel, where movement is the theme,
The wanderer's waltz is more than it may seem.
A ballet of exploration, a pas de deux with fate,
In the wanderer's waltz, the world celebrates.

"Tracks of Translation" – The Challenge of Bridging Language Barriers

On tracks of translation, where words diverge and blend,
Bridging the silence, where languages contend.
The rhythm of one tongue, a dance unfamiliar,
A challenge embraced, in the art of vernacular.

Mountains of meanings, lost in linguistic mist,
The traveler endeavors, in translation's gentle twist.
Rivers of nuances, flowing in between,
On tracks of translation, where understanding convene.

Through the labyrinth of syntax, a linguistic maze,
The challenge persists, like a cultural phrase.
In the crossroads of expressions, where meanings transpose,
Tracks of translation navigate, where empathy chose.

Each word a bridge, spanning the gap wide,
On tracks of translation, where understanding abides.
In the dialogue of tongues, where differences unfold,
Bridging language barriers, a story to be told.

Yet in the multiverse of languages, a beauty resides,
Tracks of translation, where connection abides.
In the tapestry of words, diversity's grand creation,
On tracks of translation, a harmonious narration.

"Inkwell Journeys" – The Writer's Creative Process on the Road

In the inkwell journeys, where roads and verses align,
The writer embarks on a quest, where imagination entwines.
Mountains of inspiration, peaks in creative ascent,
As the ink flows freely, on the parchment's intent.

Rivers of words carve the landscapes of the mind,
In the inkwell journeys, narratives unwind.
Cityscapes painted in metaphors and rhyme,
As the writer wanders, lost in space and time.

The journey unfolds, a literary expedition,
In the inkwell's depths, a poetic composition.
Footprints of musings on the road less traveled,
Inkwell journeys, where stories are unraveled.

Through the meandering lanes of the writer's traverse,
In the inkwell's journeys, creativity converges.
Under the starlit sky of the writer's domain,
Inkwell journeys etch tales, an endless refrain.

"Journey to Enlightenment" – Seeking Wisdom Through Worldly Experiences

On the journey to enlightenment, a quest profound,
Footsteps echo on pathways, with wisdom to be found.
Mountains stand as mentors, whispering ancient tales,
As the seeker ascends, each summit unveils.

Rivers of understanding flow with a gentle grace,
Carving channels through the mind, a reflective space.
In the city's hustle, and in nature's serene embrace,
The journey to enlightenment finds its destined place.

Beneath the canvas of the ever-changing sky,
The seeker learns, grows, and begins to fly.
Through the dance of joy and the shadows of despair,
The journey unfolds, with a wisdom rare.

In the tapestry of life, where stories intertwine,
The journey to enlightenment becomes a design.
A quest through diverse landscapes, a sacred ascent,
Seeking wisdom through experiences, the soul's enrichment.

"Verse of the Voyager" – Celebrating the Traveler's Spirit in Verse

In the verse of the voyager, a tale unfolds,
Of wanderlust's fire, where destinies are told.
Mountains become stanzas, their peaks reaching high,
As the voyager's spirit soars, beneath the vast sky.

Rivers weave rhymes, in a lyrical flow,
On the verse of the voyager, where dreams gently grow.
Cities stand as verses, in a pulsating rhyme,
Each journey, a stanza in the traveler's lifetime.

Beneath starlit verses, on roads unexplored,
The voyager's heart beats in rhythm with the chord.
Through the pages of landscapes, where stories entwine,
The verse of the voyager becomes a poetic sign.

In the canvas of horizons, where sunsets blend,
The voyager's spirit, a poetic trend.
With every step taken, a new line in the verse,
Celebrating the traveler's spirit, an ode diverse.

"Trail of Inspiration" – Finding Creative Muse in Different Places

On the trail of inspiration, where pathways intertwine,
Nature whispers sonnets, in a forest so divine.
Mountains echo verses in their stoic grandeur,
The trail of inspiration, where creativity will stir.

Rivers serenade with melodies, a liquid inspiration,
As the trail winds onward, a journey of creation.
City streets hum with the vibrancy of life,
On the trail of inspiration, where musings are rife.

Beneath the starlit canvas, where dreams take flight,
The trail of inspiration paints the poet's night.
Deserts sculpt reflections in the sands of contemplation,
A pilgrimage on the trail, seeking muse and revelation.

In every corner of the world, where footsteps dance,
The trail of inspiration offers a poetic trance.
For in the journey's cadence, a muse is found,
On the trail of inspiration, where creativity is unbound.

"Voyage of Valor" – Stories of Courage Encountered During Travel

In the voyage of valor, where courage sets sail,
On oceans of uncertainty, against the tempest's wail.
Mountains stand as witnesses, silent and grand,
As tales of courage unfurl, across the vast land.

Rivers narrate stories of fortitude, flowing free,
In the voyage of valor, where bravery meets the sea.
Through bustling city streets and quiet village lanes,
The voyage unfolds, where courage sustains.

Underneath the canvas of the star-studded night,
The voyage of valor is a beacon of light.
Footprints of resilience mark the traveler's trail,
In the tapestry of courage, where destinies prevail.

Amidst the challenges faced on the winding road,
The voyage of valor reveals the tales bestowed.
For in each courageous step taken on the way,
The journey becomes an epic, a valorous display.

"Rhymes of Revelation" – Moments of Profound Realization During a Journey

In the rhymes of revelation, on the journey's vast expanse,
Moments unfold like verses, in a cosmic dance.
Mountains become metaphors, whispering ancient tales,
As the rhymes of revelation echo through distant trails.

Rivers carve sermons in the stones they gently kiss,
In the journey's rhymes, where revelations reminisce.
City streets resonate with the pulse of realization,
The rhymes of revelation, a symphony of sensation.

Beneath the cosmic canopy, where stars inscribe their lore,
Rhymes of revelation unveil truths to explore.
Through the meandering passages of introspection,
The journey's rhymes yield profound reflection.

In the quiet moments of sunrise and twilight's glow,
Rhymes of revelation in the traveler's heart grow.
Footprints on the sand mark the tales retold,
In the rhymes of revelation, wisdom unfolds.

For in every step taken, on this journey's poetic trail,
Rhymes of revelation become whispers of the soul's unveil.
In the tapestry of time, where destinies weave,
The rhymes of revelation, profound and relieve.

"Whispers of the Wandering Heart" – Love and Longing on the Road

In the whispers of the wandering heart, love takes flight,
A serenade echoing through the quiet of the night.
Mountains stand witness to tales both near and far,
As the wandering heart seeks, beneath the moon and star.

Rivers weave verses of love, in a liquid embrace,
The wandering heart longs for a familiar face.
City lights twinkle, a dance in the twilight's hue,
As the heart wanders, searching for love that's true.

Beneath the vastness of the celestial dome,
Whispers of the wandering heart find a home.
In each stride taken on roads unknown,
Longing becomes a melody, a melancholy tone.

Through the tapestry of landscapes, where distances part,
The whispers of the wandering heart reveal a tender art.
For in the journey's cadence, where love takes its part,
The wandering heart finds solace in the whispers of the heart.

"Wanderlust's Sonata" – Music and Travel as Harmonious Experiences

In Wanderlust's Sonata, where music intertwines,
Notes become footsteps, dancing in rhythmic lines.
Mountains echo melodies, their peaks like a score,
A symphony of travel, where adventures adore.

Rivers compose ballads, flowing with grace,
Through meadows and valleys, a harmonious embrace.
City streets hum with the urban beat,
Wanderlust's Sonata, a melody so sweet.

Beneath the canvas of the vast open sky,
The wanderer listens, as the wind whispers by.
In the hush of a forest or the roar of the sea,
Wanderlust's Sonata becomes a soulful decree.

Each step taken, a note in the grand composition,
As the traveler explores, a musical transition.
Through the diversity of landscapes, a harmonious play,
Wanderlust's Sonata, where dreams find their way.

Underneath the starlit night, where silence ensues,
Wanderlust's Sonata unfolds in quiet cues.
In the journey's cadence, where music and travel meet,
A harmonious symphony, where adventures repeat.

"Trails of Triumph" – Overcoming Obstacles and Achieving Goals

On trails of triumph, where footsteps mark the way,
The journey unfolds, with the promise of a new day.
Mountains of challenges, standing tall and grand,
Yet, on trails of triumph, courage takes a stand.

Rivers of resilience flow with relentless might,
Through valleys of obstacles, under the day's soft light.
Each step, a victory, on the winding road,
On trails of triumph, where dreams are stowed.

Beneath the vast canopy, where hopes take flight,
The traveler conquers darkness, embracing the light.
In the tapestry of effort, where struggles may entwine,
Trails of triumph witness every summit climbed.

Through the city's hustle and the quiet village lane,
On trails of triumph, where resilience is gained.
In the echoes of triumph, where stories resound,
The journey continues, on trails of victory crowned.

"Quest for Serenity" – Finding Inner Peace Through Travel

In the quest for serenity, where echoes of silence play,
Travel becomes a refuge, a haven far away.
Mountains stand as sentinels, in quiet majesty,
Whispering tales of peace, an ageless symphony.

Rivers murmur tranquility, a liquid lullaby,
As the traveler seeks solace, beneath the open sky.
City streets unveil corners where calmness resides,
In the quest for serenity, where inner peace abides.

Beneath the stars' gentle glow, a cosmic retreat,
The traveler finds serenity, in nature's heartbeat.
Through the labyrinth of landscapes, where stillness is found,
The quest for serenity becomes a soulful rebound.

In the quietude of the journey, where thoughts unfold,
Serene moments become treasures, more precious than gold.
For in the traveler's heart, a tranquil decree,
The quest for serenity unfolds, a journey to be free.

"Adventures in Ascent" – Climbing Metaphorical and Literal Peaks

In adventures of ascent, where mountains rise,
Metaphorical peaks and summits to surmise.
Climbing heights both literal and within,
The journey of ascent, where victories begin.

Mountains stand as symbols, challenges embraced,
In the ascent's rhythm, where dreams are traced.
Rivers carve paths, a metaphorical climb,
As the traveler ascends, against the hands of time.

Cityscapes rise like towers, aspirations tall,
Adventures in ascent, answering the inner call.
Footsteps on rocky trails and corporate peaks,
In the ascent's narrative, where courage speaks.

Beneath the celestial canvas, stars ignite,
Adventures in ascent, where souls take flight.
Through valleys of doubt and summits of elation,
The journey of ascent, a perpetual sensation.

In the ascent's ballet, where steps align,
Adventures unfold, a dance so divine.
For in every climb, both high and low,
The spirit ascends, in a continuous flow.

"Wandering Through Wonders" – Celebrating the Marvels of the World

Wandering through wonders, where marvels unfold,
A journey through beauty, a tale to be told.
Mountains rise majestically, touching the sky,
Wonders of nature that capture the eye.

Rivers meander with a serpentine grace,
Carving landscapes in a watery embrace.
In cityscapes that glitter under the moon's soft glow,
Wonders of architecture in a vibrant show.

Forests whisper secrets in a symphony of leaves,
Wonders of green, where nature achieves.
Beneath the vast canopy of a starlit night,
Wandering through wonders, a celestial delight.

Sunsets paint canvases in hues divine,
Wonders of color that gracefully shine.
On sandy shores where waves gently kiss,
Wonders of the ocean, an eternal bliss.

In the tapestry of cultures, where stories blend,
Wonders of humanity, where connections extend.
Through the mosaic of wonders, where dreams unfurl,
A wandering heart finds a vast, wondrous world.

"Pathways of Possibility" – Embracing the Potential of New Journeys

On pathways of possibility, where horizons expand,
Footsteps echo with purpose, across uncharted land.
Mountains stand as gatekeepers, inviting the brave,
In the journey's cadence, where dreams engrave.

Rivers of potential flow with a steady grace,
Carving pathways of promise, embracing the chase.
City lights shimmer, offering tales untold,
On pathways of possibility, where destinies unfold.

Beneath the canvas of the evolving sky,
Pathways of possibility beckon the passerby.
Through the corridors of time, where futures align,
The journey unfolds, embracing the divine.

In the quiet moments where choices are spun,
Pathways of possibility gleam like the sun.
For in each step taken, a new tale is spun,
On the pathways of possibility, where dreams are won.

"Odyssey of Connection" – Stories of Forming Deep Bonds During Travel

In the odyssey of connection, where stories intertwine,
Strangers become companions, under the travel sign.
Mountains echo laughter, their peaks filled with cheer,
An odyssey of connection, where bonds draw near.

Rivers of shared moments flow in harmony,
Forging friendships in the journey's symphony.
City lights become a backdrop for tales untold,
In the odyssey of connection, where hearts unfold.

Beneath the vast celestial canvas, stars witness,
The odyssey of connection, a cosmic finesse.
Through the alleys of exploration, where footsteps align,
Deep connections form, like stars that brightly shine.

In the quietude of shared glances and smiles,
Odyssey of connection spans miles and miles.
Through cultural tapestries, where stories entwine,
In the odyssey of connection, hearts align.

For in each journey taken, where paths interlace,
Odyssey of connection becomes a sacred space.
A narrative woven in the fabric of recollection,
In the odyssey of connection, a heartfelt collection.

"Wanderer's Oath" – Pledging Loyalty to the Spirit of Exploration

In the wanderer's oath, beneath the open sky,
A pledge to exploration, where dreams will fly.
Mountains stand witness, their peaks high and grand,
As the wanderer swears to traverse every land.

Rivers bear witness to the oath's gentle flow,
A loyalty to the journey, come sun or snow.
City lights flicker, a promise in their glow,
In the wanderer's oath, a passion to bestow.

Beneath the celestial expanse, stars become the seal,
Wanderer's oath, a commitment so real.
Through valleys of wonder and deserts of discovery,
The oath resounds, a sacred odyssey.

In the whispering winds and the rustle of leaves,
Wanderer's oath binds, as the soul believes.
For in every step taken, a pledge to the roam,
Wanderer's oath echoes, a traveler's solemn home.

"Tracks of Togetherness" – The Joy of Traveling with Loved Ones

On tracks of togetherness, where love takes the lead,
A journey with loved ones, a bond to heed.
Mountains witness laughter, their peaks echoing delight,
Tracks of togetherness, where hearts unite.

Rivers of shared memories flow in a serene embrace,
Carving pathways of joy, leaving a lasting trace.
Cityscapes become a canvas for stories untold,
On tracks of togetherness, where warmth unfolds.

Beneath the vast canvas of the twilight sky,
Tracks of togetherness, where connections multiply.
Through winding roads and open fields,
The journey with loved ones, its joy reveals.

In the quiet moments where laughter rings,
Tracks of togetherness, like music sings.
For in each shared adventure, a treasure is found,
On the tracks of togetherness, where love is bound.

"Inkwell Reveries" – The Poet's Daydreams While on the Road

In the inkwell reveries, on roads less traveled,
The poet's daydreams in verses unraveled.
Mountains become musings, their peaks reaching high,
In inkwell reveries, where fantasies fly.

Rivers whisper tales in a liquid cadence,
As the poet daydreams, lost in the essence.
City streets unravel stories untold,
In the inkwell reveries, where imagination unfolds.

Beneath the canvas of the ever-changing sky,
Inkwell reveries paint dreams that never die.
Through the tapestry of landscapes, the poet roams,
In daydreams inked in stanzas, the poet composes.

In the quietude of nature and urban strife,
Inkwell reveries breathe life into life.
For in every line written, the poet conceives,
A world in inkwell reveries, where the soul believes.

"Journey to Wholeness" – Seeking Completeness Through Travel Experiences

On the journey to wholeness, where fragments align,
Travel becomes the catalyst, a path to define.
Mountains stand as symbols, reaching for the sky,
In the journey to wholeness, where souls learn to fly.

Rivers flow with purpose, a liquid metaphor,
Carving through obstacles, as the journey explores.
City lights twinkle, a mosaic of dreams,
On the journey to wholeness, where unity gleams.

Beneath the celestial tapestry, where stars converse,
The journey to wholeness is a universe.
Through the crossroads of encounters and diverse scenes,
In the journey to wholeness, completeness convenes.

For in each step taken, a puzzle piece found,
On the journey to wholeness, where self is unbound.
A tapestry woven with threads so fine,
In the journey to wholeness, where destinies entwine.

"Verse of the Vagabond" – The Nomadic Perspective on Life

In the verse of the vagabond, a nomadic refrain,
Footsteps echo, a melody on the open terrain.
Mountains become stanzas, their peaks reaching high,
In the nomad's verse, where the free spirits fly.

Rivers weave stories, a liquid narrative,
Carving tales on the landscapes, where dreams live.
City lights flicker like verses in the night,
In the vagabond's poem, where wanderers find light.

Beneath the starlit canvas, where the moon takes command,
The verse of the vagabond, a journey so grand.
Through the tapestry of cultures, where stories converse,
In the nomad's verse, diverse narratives disperse.

In the solitude of deserts and forests unknown,
Verse of the vagabond, a ballad on its own.
For every sunrise witnessed and every sunset adored,
The nomad's verse is written, a testament explored.

In the pages of travel, where destinations blend,
Verse of the vagabond, an odyssey without end.
Through the cadence of nomadic life's rhyming bond,
In the verse of the vagabond, the wanderer responds.

"Trail of Testimony" – Bearing Witness to the World's Beauty and Challenges

On the trail of testimony, where footsteps align,
Bearing witness to the world's beauty and design.
Mountains stand as witnesses, grand and tall,
Testifying tales, in their silent sprawl.

Rivers bear witness, flowing through the land,
Carrying stories of life, both grand and bland.
City streets testify to the pulse of the urban heart,
In the trail of testimony, where stories impart.

Beneath the vast canvas of the celestial dome,
Testimonies unfold, stories etched in stone.
Through the labyrinth of nature and bustling town,
In the trail of testimony, where destinies are sown.

In the quiet corners where shadows play,
Trail of testimony, where echoes stay.
For every sunrise witnessed and every storm braved,
The trail of testimony, where life's stories are engraved.

In the pages of time, where history is drawn,
Trail of testimony, a witness to the dawn.
Through the journey's cadence, both beauty and trial,
In the trail of testimony, the world's narrative compiles.

"Voyage of Visions" – The Dreams and Goals that come to Life Through Travel

In the voyage of visions, where dreams set sail,
Goals become stars, in the traveler's tale.
Mountains stand as mentors, guiding the way,
In the voyage of visions, where aspirations sway.

Rivers flow with purpose, mirroring the dream,
Carving paths of ambition, where possibilities gleam.
Cityscapes become canvases for dreams to unfold,
In the voyage of visions, where stories are told.

Beneath the celestial canopy, stars whisper hope,
Voyage of visions, where dreams elope.
Through the landscapes of ambition, where destinies align,
In the voyage of visions, dreams intertwine.

In the quiet moments of reflection, where the heart envisions,
Voyage of visions becomes life's decisions.
For every step taken toward the dream's embrace,
In the voyage of visions, reality finds its place.

"Rhymes of Reconciliation" – Finding Peace and Resolution During a Journey

In the rhymes of reconciliation, where echoes find a song,
Journeys unfold, where healing does belong.
Mountains stand as witnesses, majestic and serene,
Rhymes of reconciliation, where past wounds convene.

Rivers weave tales of forgiveness in their flowing stream,
Carrying hopes and resolutions, like a sacred dream.
City streets resonate with the rhythm of accord,
In the rhymes of reconciliation, where peace is stored.

Beneath the vastness of the twilight's soft hue,
Rhymes of reconciliation, where understanding grew.
Through the tapestry of landscapes, where differences
combine,
The journey becomes a poem, a harmony divine.

In the quiet corners of self-discovery,
Rhymes of reconciliation unveil the tapestry.
For every step taken on the path of grace,
Rhymes of reconciliation find a resting place.

In the cadence of time, where resolutions chime,
Rhymes of reconciliation become a soothing rhyme.
Through the journey's verses, where conflicts cease,
Rhymes of reconciliation bring a lasting peace.

"Whispers of the Weary" – The Rest and Respite Sought During Travel

In the whispers of the weary, a travelogue unfolds,
Seeking rest and respite, where weariness molds.
Mountains stand as guardians, their peaks a tranquil retreat,
Whispers of the weary, where solace and rest meet.

Rivers murmur lullabies, inviting sleep's embrace,
Carrying the whispers of the weary to a tranquil space.
City lights dim, a soft glow in the night,
In the whispers of the weary, seeking respite.

Beneath the canvas of stars, where night softly weaves,
Whispers of the weary find solace in the eaves.
Through the tapestry of landscapes, where tired souls roam,
In the whispers of the weary, a sanctuary is found.

In the quietude of moments where shadows play,
Whispers of the weary lead to a peaceful bay.
For every tired step taken on the winding road,
Whispers of the weary find refuge and abode.

—— ⟩⟨ ——

"Wanderlust's Symphony" – The Harmonious Blending of Cultures on the Road

In Wanderlust's Symphony, a global concerto unfolds,
Harmonies of cultures, stories beautifully told.
Mountains become notes, peaks reaching high,
In the symphony of wanderlust, where unity lies.

Rivers flow with melodies, a liquid embrace,
Carrying the tunes of diverse lands, in rhythmic grace.
Cityscapes join the orchestra, a bustling refrain,
Wanderlust's Symphony, a cultural terrain.

Beneath the celestial canopy, stars softly play,
Symphony of wanderlust, where night turns to day.
Through the mosaic of languages, where voices entwine,
In the harmonious blend, cultural chords combine.

In the city squares and distant village greens,
Wanderlust's Symphony, a symphony of scenes.
For in every step taken on this global stage,
Wanderlust's Symphony creates a harmonious page.

"Trails of Timelessness" – Experiencing Moments that Seem Eternal

On trails of timelessness, where moments stretch and sway,
Eternity unfolds, in the beauty of the day.
Mountains stand as sentinels, witnesses to the sublime,
Trails of timelessness, where each second is a rhyme.

Rivers whisper tales of ages in a gentle flow,
Carving paths of time, where memories grow.
City lights sparkle, caught in a temporal dance,
In trails of timelessness, where chance finds its chance.

Beneath the canvas of the ever-changing sky,
Trails of timelessness, where past and present lie.
Through the meandering lanes of experience and delight,
The journey becomes timeless, in the traveler's sight.

In the quiet moments when the world stands still,
Trails of timelessness weave stories at will.
For in every heartbeat and every breath we take,
Trails of timelessness, an eternal journey makes.

"Quest for Discovery" – The Insatiable Desire to Uncover New Places

In the quest for discovery, where horizons enthrall,
Footsteps echo a rhythm, answering the wanderer's call.
Mountains beckon with mysteries, their peaks high,
In the quest for discovery, where dreams touch the sky.

Rivers meander through landscapes yet untold,
Carrying the whispers of tales, in a liquid fold.
City streets unfold stories in their vibrant sprawl,
In the quest for discovery, where wonders install.

Beneath the vast tapestry of the celestial dome,
Quest for discovery, a desire to freely roam.
Through uncharted territories, where the heart leads,
The journey becomes a map, with dreams as seeds.

In the quiet moments where newness takes root,
Quest for discovery, an insatiable pursuit.
For every discovery, a chapter unfurls,
In the quest for discovery, where the heart swirls.

"Adventures in Harmony" – The Unity Found in Diversity During Travel

In adventures in harmony, diversity unfolds,
A tapestry woven with stories yet untold.
Mountains stand tall, a symbol of unity,
In the harmonious journey, where souls roam free.

Rivers intertwine, their currents coalesce,
Carrying the essence of unity, a liquid caress.
Cityscapes blend colors in a vibrant spree,
In adventures in harmony, where cultures agree.

Beneath the canvas of the sky's vast dome,
Adventures in harmony find a welcoming home.
Through the mosaic of languages and diverse faces,
The journey becomes a symphony, in diverse embraces.

In the quiet moments where differences align,
Adventures in harmony, a blend so divine.
For in every step taken, a dance of unity,
In the adventures of harmony, where hearts find serenity.

"Wandering Through Wisdom" – Learning from Different Cultures and Experiences

Wandering through wisdom, where cultures convene,
Footsteps echo lessons, the traveler's keen.
Mountains share stories, etched in ancient stone,
In the journey of wisdom, where insights are sown.

Rivers whisper teachings in their liquid flow,
Carrying knowledge from places unknown.
City streets narrate histories untold,
In the wandering through wisdom, where perspectives unfold.

Beneath the vast expanse of the celestial dome,
Wandering through wisdom, the traveler finds home.
Through diverse landscapes and varied scenes,
In the journey of wisdom, where understanding gleans.

In the marketplaces, where voices resonate,
Wandering through wisdom, where tales captivate.
For every encounter with a foreign face,
Wisdom becomes a guide in the traveler's embrace.

In quiet temples and bustling squares,
Wandering through wisdom, where enlightenment declares.
Through the symphony of languages and cultural rhymes,
The journey of wisdom unfolds in myriad times.

For in every step taken, a lesson blooms,
Wandering through wisdom, where knowledge looms.
In the vast library of life's vast kingdom,
The traveler discovers, wandering through wisdom.

"Pathways of Passion" – The Fervor and Excitement of the Traveler

On pathways of passion, where fervor takes flight,
Footsteps echo with excitement, pure and bright.
Mountains stand witness to the traveler's zeal,
In the pathways of passion, where dreams appeal.

Rivers flow with a spirited dance,
Carrying the traveler's fervent advance.
City lights twinkle, mirroring the heart's desire,
On pathways of passion, where passion sets afire.

Beneath the starlit canvas, where wishes soar,
Pathways of passion, an ecstatic tour.
Through the diverse landscapes where enthusiasm weaves,
The journey becomes a tapestry, where passion conceives.

In the quiet moments of self-discovery,
Pathways of passion reveal a traveler's glee.
For in every step taken, fervor's mark is cast,
On pathways of passion, where the heart beats fast.

"Odyssey of Understanding" – Gaining Insight into the Human Experience

In the odyssey of understanding, where stories unfold,
Footsteps echo lessons, the human experience retold.
Mountains stand as parables, etching tales in stone,
In the odyssey of understanding, where empathy is grown.

Rivers carry narratives in a liquid embrace,
Carving through cultures, in a diverse chase.
City streets resonate with the pulse of humanity,
In the odyssey of understanding, where hearts find unity.

Beneath the celestial expanse, where stars converse,
Odyssey of understanding, a path to traverse.
Through the labyrinth of emotions and varied scenes,
The journey becomes an insight, in vibrant sheens.

In the quiet moments where empathy sparks,
Odyssey of understanding, where compassion embarks.
For every encounter with joy, grief, or demand,
Odyssey of understanding, a journey to understand.

In the pages of time, where destinies align,
Odyssey of understanding, a narrative to define.
Through the diverse chapters of the human arc,
The odyssey unfolds, leaving a profound mark.

"Wanderer's Lighthouse" – Finding Guidance and Direction During Travel

In the wanderer's lighthouse, a beacon aglow,
Guiding the traveler where the unknown currents flow.
Mountains become pillars, steadfast and tall,
Wanderer's lighthouse, illuminating the call.

Rivers carve pathways, following the light's lead,
In the wanderer's lighthouse, where destinies feed.
City lights flicker, like stars on the shore,
Wanderer's lighthouse, a compass evermore.

Beneath the vast canopy, where constellations converse,
Wanderer's lighthouse, a celestial hearse.
Through the winding roads and uncharted seas,
The journey unfolds, guided by the breeze.

In the quiet moments, where shadows retreat,
Wanderer's lighthouse, a guide through defeat.
For every step taken in the twilight's embrace,
Wanderer's lighthouse, a steadfast grace.

"Tracks of Transformation" – How Travel Alters One's Perspective and Life

On tracks of transformation, where journeys commence,
Footprints mark the metamorphosis, the traveler's recompense.
Mountains become mentors, guiding the way,
In the tracks of transformation, where perspectives sway.

Rivers whisper secrets of change in their flowing spree,
Carrying the tales of evolution, setting spirits free.
City lights twinkle, reflecting the altered view,
On tracks of transformation, where life begins anew.

Beneath the vast celestial expanse, where stars align,
Tracks of transformation, a cosmic design.
Through landscapes of self-discovery and change,
The journey reshapes, a kaleidoscope so strange.

In the quiet moments, where introspection dwells,
Tracks of transformation weave stories that tell.
For in every step taken, a life rearranged,
Tracks of transformation, where perspectives are exchanged.